The Whirlwind Journal

Tris Yu

Presentation by *BookLeaf Publishing*

Web: www.bookleafpub.com

E-mail: info@bookleafpub.com

ISBN: 9789395784658

First edition 2023

DEDICATION

To my hot air balloon that encourages my mind to soar but keeps me grounded always, and will always gently embrace me no matter how ugly or beautiful my thoughts are.

PREFACE

The writing started shortly after starting a long distance relationship. I felt love in a way I have never before, yet brought about insecurities and memories of a painful past. This experience was full of love and pain for me, and I have always documented my emotions in the form of poetry or short writing. I wanted to have an outlet for my overwhelming pain and love. This might be too personal, might not be relatable, but these poems were written with all my heart.

rough waters

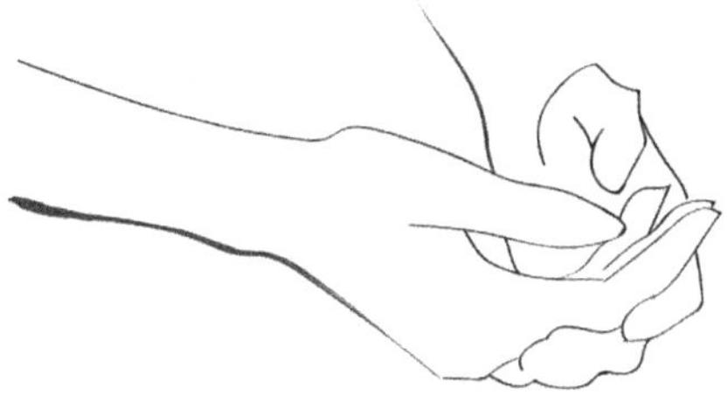

tide after tide
waves pull me under
i sink and struggle to breathe
losing hope that I could swim back above
your hand reached for mine
i almost forgot you were
always there ready to save me
i am never alone with your love

feeling the distance

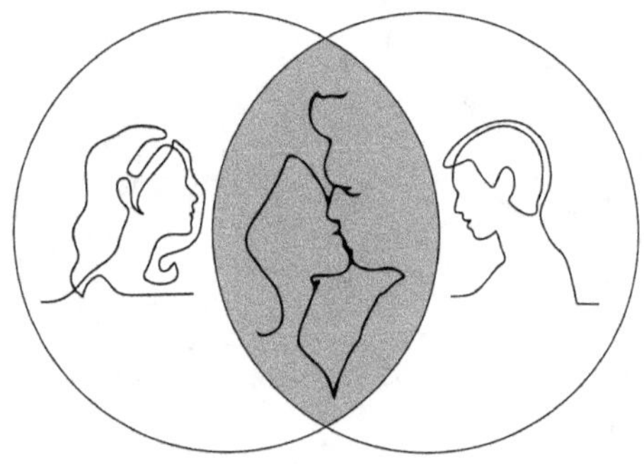

it's like night and day
our days and nights
grasp onto every waking moment
with time I fight
hours apart and miles away
try as I might
to keep myself from shattering
with no one in sight

too empty to bleed

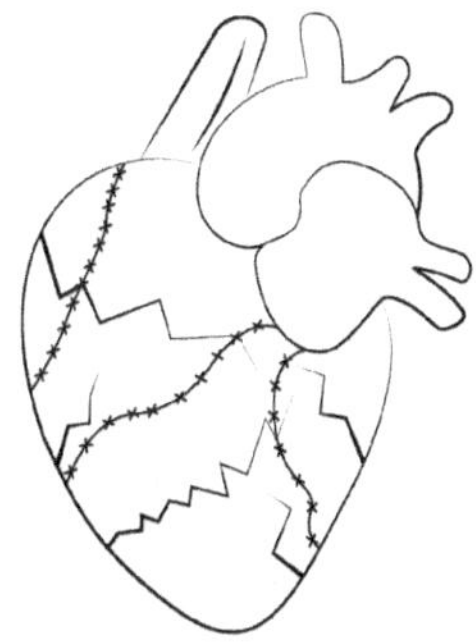

loneliness
emptiness
aching and reaching
hole in heart gaping
grip and tear it wide open
wretched urges worsen
self-destruction
no direction

no happily ever after

you said you would embrace my flaws
so did they, till they chose to claw
my heart out, the damage is what you saw

you said you would not leave like the others
so did they, till like a change in weather
i was left alone to wilt and wither

you said you would give me my happily ever
after
so did they, till i ceased to matter
i am afraid you will also make me shatter

do you know me

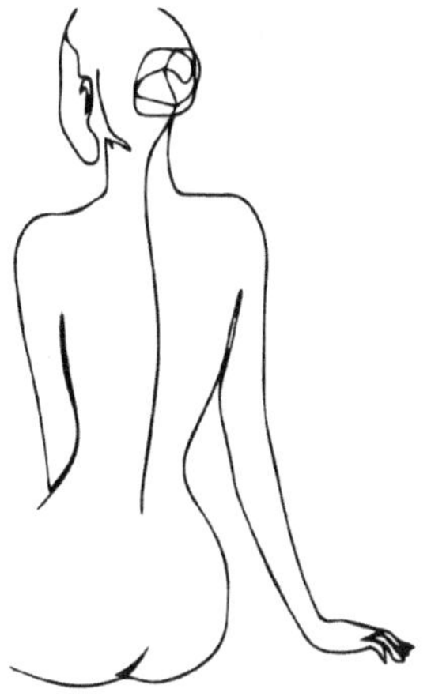

once the high wears off
and you pull off the cloth
that's been masking everything beneath
that's ugly, and you'll want to leave

to the ones who left me in ruins

you're just a liar
bent me to your desire
left me with one flat tire
setting all our plans on fire

and did you ever feel sorry
for my love that you buried
this isn't a party, where more is merry
the one who's unwanted, this burden I'll carry

you

you are not here
yet you are everywhere
in the cool breeze
in the warmth under my blankets
in my favorite song playing in the mall
in the books i read
in a sip of hot chocolate

my daydreams and midnight musings
all lead back to you
i close my eyes
all i see is
you

twin flame

you, me, two halves of a whole
you, me, our lives took a toll
the worst in you, the worst in me
set love on fire, from ashes we flee

soulmate

from ashes i fled
the tears i shed
the pain i endured, to growth it led
no longer one half, whole on my own
though my soul shattered, my heart, stone
light shown through when i was all alone
i did not need you, nor you, me
and love is not math, as you can see
one plus one is not two, but free

relief

fresh breath of air
when i didn't realize
i forgot to breathe
alive again
when i didn't realize
i was dead inside
whole
when i didn't realize
i was shattered all along

what is

i always thought
to be in love
is to always be happy
until you

to be in love
i found
is to be happy
maybe upset
or angry
but always wishing for your happiness
always choosing you
over and over again

what i want with you
is not just happiness
but to feel with you
everything in life

being in love with you
is feeling alive
with you

extremes

did you know
i am only an angel
sweet, kind, gentle
when there's light
for there is a part of me that's
a devil
dirty, wretched, sinful
lurking in the dark
if you only knew
all the filthy thoughts in my head
when the night falls
will you still be there
when the day comes

r u happy

i ask myself
every night before bed
if i died in my sleep
would i die happy
if i thought i'd die happy
why did death cross my mind
like it was easy

hair

haircut
after a breakup
no

but
from brown and blond
vibrant for you
i dye my hair back
dark and natural
streaks of purple
my favorite color
before you

i won't erase you
but i will remember
how i found myself
in the ruins you left behind

insatiable

i knew within me
there will always be this raw hunger left
unsatisfied
how could it
when it
and it alone
contradicts all the other things
i look for in life

too late

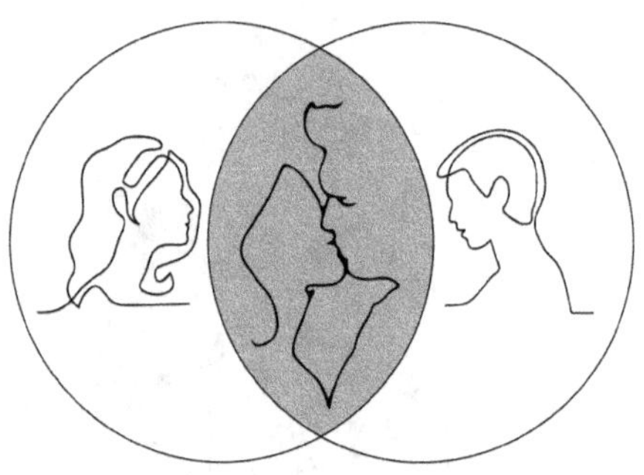

a bit of darkness
jealousy and possessiveness
spark
that i haven't felt in years
lit up my lonely path

there's never been another like this
you'll never find another like this
do you mean it
have i moved you
the way you've moved me

because
now that you made a spark
passion set ablaze
it's too late to walk away
from the flames of my wretched soul

novel

like my favorite novel
that i will read over and over again
and love so much
that i will never get bored of

writing

i wrote so much about you
yet it's always so difficult
to find the right words
because there are no right words

you feel too right
that everything that i say
feels so wrong

the more i love you
the less i know

fear

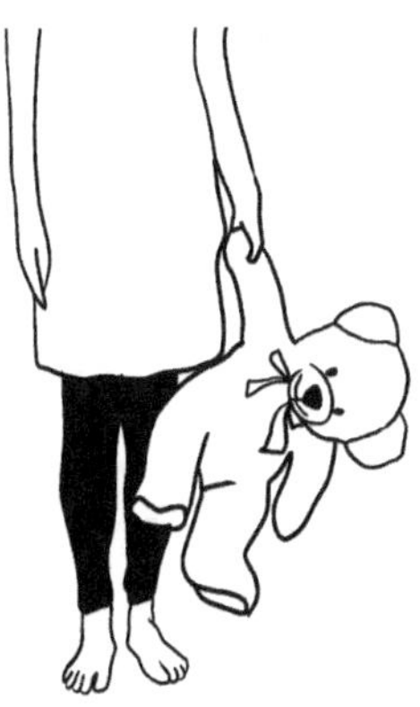

i don't think i have ever
feared anything as much

i have never feared
people leaving my life

i have always been indifferent

until you
you made me feel
the fear of losing someone

the fear of losing you

a little

why is it so difficult

wishing
timezones a little less distant
distance a little less apart
heart a little less fragile

would i be able to finally reach you
hold you
feel you

fortnight

you did you know
right now
my dreams and reality
are only a fortnight apart

time is finally bringing me
closer to you

9.9.2022